John Horne Tooke

Facts

addressed to the landlords, stockholders, merchants, farmers, manufacturers, tradesmen, proprietors of every description, and generally to all the subjects of Great Britain and Ireland. Sixth Edition

John Horne Tooke

Facts
addressed to the landlords, stockholders, merchants, farmers, manufacturers, tradesmen, proprietors of every description, and generally to all the subjects of Great Britain and Ireland. Sixth Edition

ISBN/EAN: 9783337311568

Printed in Europe, USA, Canada, Australia, Japan

Cover: Foto ©Andreas Hilbeck / pixelio.de

More available books at **www.hansebooks.com**

FACTS:

ADDRESSED TO THE

LANDHOLDERS,	FARMERS,
STOCKHOLDERS,	MANUFACTURERS,
MERCHANTS,	TRADESMEN,

PROPRIETORS OF EVERY DESCRIPTION,

AND GENERALLY TO ALL

THE SUBJECTS OF GREAT BRITAIN AND IRELAND.

UBI DOLOR, IBI DIGITUS.

THE SIXTH EDITION.

LONDON:
PRINTED FOR J. JOHNSON, N°. 72, ST. PAUL's
CHURCH-YARD, and J. ALMON, in PICCADILLY, 1780.

To the Landholders, Stockholders, Merchants, Farmers, Manufacturers, Tradesmen, Proprietors of every Description, and generally to all the Subjects of Great Britain and Ireland.

Fellow Countrymen,

IT was only by the death of one king and the expulsion of another, by a long train of cruel civil wars, and a deluge of the best blood in the country, that our ancestors could at length obtain from *prerogative*, that the judges (who only *declare the law*) should no longer be under the corrupt influence and power of the crown. And, though costly, they thought the purchase wisely made.

What is now OUR struggle?

That those who *make the laws* shall no longer be prostituted to infamous, and sordid gain: that the legislature itself may be rescued from temptations which flesh and blood cannot withstand.

The violence of *prerogative* diverted the streams of justice, and turned the course of them from their natural and ordinary channel; yet when the hand of violence was taken off, when the dam of prerogative was removed, the streams ran clear and purer than before. But the corruption of Parliament is not merely a turning of the course, it is a poisoning of the water at the fountain-head.

"The integrity of Parliament (it has been well observed) is the key-stone that keeps the whole together. If this be shaken, our constitution totters: if it be quite removed, our constitution falls into ruin."

Is it then only *shaken?*

Is it not quite *removed?*

Have not three or four hundred mercenaries in the two Houses already effected against the prosperity and liberties of this country,

INTRODUCTION.

country, what ten times as many thousands out of them would have attempted in vain?

Our ancestors have shut up, with all the bars and bolts of law, the principal entries through which *prerogative* could burst in upon us. It is ours to close the avenue of corruption, through which the *influence of the Crown* now threatens our final ruin.

To direct your attention to the true source of all our evils, and to the only means of our salvation, it is thought proper to lay before you the three following MOTIONS; accompanied with some notorious and incontestable FACTS, which admit neither of denial nor of palliation; and which whilst they evidence the justice of our complaints, and the intolerable enormity of our grievances, do at the same time point out both the necessity and means of a thorough and speedy reformation.

CHAP.

CHAP. I.

MOTIONS LATELY MADE IN THE HOUSE OF LORDS.

THE *First* is a Motion of his Grace the Duke of Richmond; who, on Tuesday, December 7, 1779, moved,

" THAT an humble address be presented to his Majesty, to beseech his Majesty to reflect on the manifold distresses, and difficulties in which this kingdom is involved, too deeply felt to stand in need of enumeration.

" To represent that amidst the many, and various matters which require reformation, and must undergo correction before this country can rise superior to its powerful enemies, the waste of public treasure requires instant remedy. That profusion is not vigour; and that it is become indispensably necessary to adopt that true œconomy which, by reforming all useless expences, creates confidence in Government, gives energy to its exertions, and provides the means for their continuance, humbly to submit to his Majesty, that a considerable reduction of his Majesty's *Civil List* would be an example well becoming his Majesty's paternal affection for his people, and his own dignity; could not fail of diffusing its influence through every department of the state, and would add true lustre to his crown, from the grateful feelings of a distressed people.

" To assure his Majesty that this House will readily concur in promoting so desirable a purpose; and that every one of its members will chearfully submit to such reduction of emolument in any office he may hold, as his Majesty in his royal wisdom may think proper to make."

The *Second* is a Motion of the Earl of Shelburne; who, on Wednesday, December 15, 1779, moved,

" THAT the alarming addition annually making to the present enormous national debt, under the head of *extraordinaries* incurred in the different services, requires
im-

immediate check and controul.—The increasing the public expence beyond the grants of Parliament being at all times an invasion of the fundamental rights of Parliament, and the utmost œconomy being indispensably necessary in the present reduced and deplorable state of the landed and mercantile interest of Great Britain, and Ireland."

The *Third* is a Motion of the Earl of Shelburne, who, on Wednesday, December 15, 1779, moved,

" THAT the Lords be summoned for *Tuesday, the 8th of February next*, to take into consideration a motion.—That a Committee be appointed, consisting of Members of both Houses, possessing neither employment nor pension, to examine without delay into the public expenditure and the mode of accounting for the same: more particularly into the manner of making all contracts, and at the same time to take into consideration, what saving can be made consistent with public dignity, justice and gratitude, by an abolition of old and new created

created offices, the duties of which have either ceased, or shall on enquiry prove inadequate to the fees, or other emoluments arising therefrom; or by the reduction of such salaries, or other allowances and profits as may appear to be unreasonable: that the same may be applied to lessen the present ruinous expenditure, and to enable us to carry on the present war against the House of Bourbon, with that decision and vigour which can alone result from national zeal, confidence, and unanimity."

The propriety of the *First* motion will most evidently appear, by considering that in the early times of our constitution, the whole expence of the state was borne by the crown; aided indeed sometimes by the people, when they approved the occasion of the expence; and if the king was then vested with the sole power of appointing to offices, and of declaring and conducting war; it is likewise certain that those officers of state were indeed at that time literally *his* servants, paid out of *his* coffers, and disposing of *his* treasure: and that together with the chief burden of war, the misconduct or miscarriage of it affected, in the first place and principally, the king himself.

The same power has continued in the crown, though the reason of it has ceased. The *people* now bear the whole burden and expence both of the civil government and of war. They alone suffer all the consequences of misconduct and miscarriage; although the crown exclusively appoints the ministers to whom such misconduct and miscarriage can alone be imputed. The king's private revenue (drawn from the pockets of his people) is now fixed and certain: his comparative domestic riches, therefore, and power become greater in proportion to the increasing poverty of his subjects. Not only so, but in the present unexampled expensive war, his private revenue has received an unexampled increase.—Is it any thing but justice then, that his income should, at least, partake the burdens and sufferings of his people, and conform in some measure to the decreased ability of his subjects, and to the diminution of the numbers of those whose

whose labours assisted in his support? More especially when we consider that this enormous *civil list* is divided amongst those very men whose votes and counsels have deprived us of three millions of industrious fellow-subjects, who toiled in common with ourselves for his greatness: for, most true it is, the king subsists by the field that is tilled; it is the labour of the people that supports the crown.

The aim of the *second* motion is to take away from Ministers, more dangerous because unlimited *civil lists,* which in the *Army* and *Navy* departments alone (exclusive of the *Ordnance*) amount at present to Six Millions a year.

The *extraordinaries of the Army* (Lord North's *civil list*) sufficiently account for our present disgraceful situation;—useless to our friends, contemptible to our enemies, and incapable of undertaking any great design, either at home or abroad; for our Ministers, it is plain, have carried on *their* war like their savage allies, whose incursions are never made to extend the dominions of their country, but to levy contributions for themselves:

only with this difference, that *our savages* have neglected their enemies to plunder their countrymen.

The *extraordinaries of the Navy* (Lord Sandwich's *civil lift*) speak plainly enough both for themselves, and for *him*. We need only to look at their amount; and then to compare the present condition of our fleets with the description given of them by his Majesty himself, in his first speech from the throne.—" As my Navy is the principal article of our natural strength, it gives me much satisfaction to *receive it in such good condition:* whilst the fleet of France is weakened to such a degree, that the small remains of it have continued *blocked up by my ships in their own ports.*"

November 16, 1760.

The *third* motion is directed against our only *natural* enemies, against the most formidable allies of the house of Bourbon; —*fraudulent contractors, useless placemen, unworthy pensioners.*—These are the fatal troops which have baffled the forces of this kingdom. By depriving the state of its revenue, they have destroyed its power.

And

And whilst they have been voting away the liberties of the people, and the dignity of parliament, they have effectually extinguished the king's real greatness; which consists not in a corrupt dominion over his subjects at home; but in the honourable influence which he ought to have upon states abroad. A king of Great Britain should be great, even amongst kings; and able, by the wisdom and authority of his counsels, so to incline and dispose the affairs of other states and nations, and those great events which sometimes happen in the world, as that all should ultimately contribute to the benefit of mankind in general, and to the peculiar honour and advantage of his own people.

But why should we dwell upon the greatness of a *king*, when the very existence of the *nation* is at stake. If there yet remains an individual in the kingdom unsasatisfied (we will not say of the *propriety* but) of the absolute *necessity* of the proposed reformation; let him seriously peruse the following FACTS.

CHAP.

CHAP. II.

Expence of the War even suppofing a Peace had been settled at Chriftmas 1779.

NOTHING can more forcibly prove the extreme neceffity of the propofed reformation, than an exhibition of the expence already incurred by the war, even with the fuppofition of an immediate peace.

The public have therefore here laid before them the expence of the prefent war, even fuppofing a peace were at this moment fettled.

	Principal.	Annual Expence.
Additional ftock of 3 per cent. annuities, in 1776	2,150,000	64,500
Four per cent. ftock with an annuity of ¼ per cent. or 25,000 l. for ten years annexed—in 1777	5,000,000	225,000
Additional 3 per cent ftock with an annuity of 2½ per cent. or 150,000 l. for 30 years—in 1778	6,000,000	330,000
Carried over	13,150,000	619,000

At Chriſtmas, 1779.   15

	Principal.	Annual Expence.
Brought over	13,150,000	619,500
Additional 3 per cent. ſtock with 3¼ per cent. or 262,500l. per ann. for 29 years annexed—in 1779	7,000,000	472,500
Value of 25,000l. per ann. for 7 years at 6	150,000	
Value of 150,000l. per ann. for 28 years, at 15	2,250,000	
Value of 262,500l. per ann. for 28 years, at 15	3,937,500	
Added to the *funded* debt ſince 1775	26,487,500	1,092,000

Unfunded Debt, on January 1, 1780.

Navy debt	8,000,000
Extraordinaries of the army (*a*)	3,100,000
Extraordinaries of the ordnance	550,000
Exchequer bills	3,400,000
Debt of the ſinking fund (*b*)	700,000
Carried over	15,750,000

(*a*) The extraordinaries of the army laſt year were 3,026,137l.

The extraordinaries of the ordnance were 521,935l. It is probable they will be more this year.

(*b*) The ſinking fund at Chriſtmas, 1778, was in debt nearly the whole Lady-Day quarter. This year, beſides providing 2,071,854l. for the ſupplies, it has this debt

Expence of the War

	Principal.	Annual Expence.
Brought over	15,750,000	
Continuance of pay to forces by sea and land, calling home troops, and other expences of war which cannot immediately cease with the war (*c*)	3,500,000	
Total *unfunded* debt	19,250,000	
Add *funded* debt	26,487,500	
	45,737,500	
Deduct the *unfunded* debt before the war	3,100,000	
Remains *addition* to the debt by the war, at Christmas, 1779	42,637,500	
Add one shilling in the pound land-tax, for four years at 450,000 l. per ann.	1,800,000	
Carried over	44,437,000	

debt to discharge; all the deficiencies of the new taxes to make good, and about 160,000 l. of the interest of this year's loan to pay. The probability therefore is that it will be as much in debt at Christmas, 1779, as it was at Christmas, 1778.—It should be further considered that ever since 1777, its produce has been falling.

(*c*) This was the sum to which these expences amounted at the peace, in 1763.—Mr. Hartley has estimated them at no less a sum than *ten millions*.

At Christmas, 1779.

	Principal.	Annual Expence.
Brought over	44,437,500	
Add the peace surplus in the revenue before the war, and applied to the expence of the war, reckoned 750,000l. per ann. including 150,000l. from annual lotteries	3,000,000	
Whole expence of the war at Christmas 1779	47,437,500	
Annual expence incurred by the *funded* debt		1,092,000
Annual expence to be incurred by funding sixteen millions (now unfunded) at 5 per cent.		800,000
Total annual expence already incurred by the war		1,892,000

Supposing the war be continued (as Mr. Eden says it probably will) for *years*; it cannot add less every year to our debt than *thirteen millions*, exclusive of the monstrous expence of *douceurs*.

In order to raise *ten millions* after Christmas, 1779 *(f)* (over and above the contribution,

―――――――――――――――――――――
(f) The loan of 1779 (including 1,400,000l. Exchequer bills lately issued) is 8,400,000l.—There is already

bution of the East-India Company) NEW TAXES, which will produce 700,000l. *per annum* must be imposed upon the people.

---

already voted for 1780, an *increased* expence of above a million. Probably therefore the loan of this year must be *ten millions*, exclusive of any provision for the *Navy Debt*.

In 1778 the *Navy Debt* increased *two millions*; and at Christmas 1778 amounted to 5,179,000l.

At Christmas 1779, it was near *eight millions*; and therefore will have increased above two millions and an half in the year.

To prevent a further increase, two millions and an half should be paid in 1780: and this would make the whole debt provided for in this year *twelve millions and an half*. It is possible however that Lord North may satisfy himself with paying off only a million of the navy debt. But this will be very bad policy: for the consequence will be, that the navy debt in 1780 will increase to *nine*, or *ten* millions; and navy bills will fall to a discount that will bear down all the public securities; and render the expence of the navy, already exorbitant, much more so.

It is said that ten millions are to be procured by selling a 3 per cent. stock at 58½ per cent. with an annuity annexed of 4 per cent. for 28 years, valued at 10⅝ years purchase, though really worth near 15 years purchase. Funds therefore must be found which will produce 700,000l. per ann.—The extravagance of this scheme is enormous: It is the same thing as procuring 5,850,000l. by selling a 3 per cent. stock at 58½; and

At Christmas, 1779.

people. In order to raise *thirteen millions* the following year, NEW TAXES, which will produce at least, 800,000l. *per annum*, must again be laid upon the people. And still *greater taxes* must be laid upon them two years hence.

The kingdom is already so loaded, and at the same time so weakened by the loss of its *dependencies*, that nothing can terrify if this does not. We know very well that *Taxes* equal to those sums may be easily *imagined*.——Adding another *three shillings* per barrel to the tax upon *beer*, together with a saving in the interest of nineteen millions which will take place a year hence would provide funds for the loan of the current year.——Mortgaging one shilling

the remainder necessary to make up ten millions (i. e. 4,150,000l.) by selling a 3 per cent. stock at 35, for $10\frac{1}{2}$ is the true value of an annuity for 28 years, when the 3 per cents are at 35. At the same time the public is bound by this scheme to pay at redemption $41\frac{1}{4}$ per cent. i. e. above *four millions* more than the money borrowed. Such is the bargain which, it is said, Lord North is to make for the public. But possibly he may chuse to make the *douceur a long annuity:* and, in that case, funds which will produce 600,000l. per ann. will be sufficient to pay the *interest* of the loan.

shilling in the pound of the land-tax, together with taxes upon *saddles, lawyers, tickets for plays, bricks, successions to estates,* &c. And all the remaining *gleanings* of taxes possible to be collected, might perhaps furnish funds for borrowing *thirteen* millions the next year.—Also, *doubling the window tax,* adding *another 5 per cent.* to the excises and customs and *tripling* the *coach tax,* and *servant's tax* might furnish funds for a *third* year. But all this is chimerical, and wild.

It should be remembered, that there is a limit beyond which taxation cannot be carried with effect. Taxes, when they become too burthensome, will be evaded. They will lessen consumption; destroy trade; encroach upon one another; engender rage; and terminate in revolt. It will be strange if two or three years more of the present war do not bring us to this crisis.—Sixty years ago *one half* of the present taxes, and *a third* of the present debt, were reckoned a burden almost intolerable. Our increase of strength has been owing partly to the increase of commerce; but principally to the increase of our

At Christmas, 1779.

our *paper money*: the ability to pay taxes being always in proportion to the quantity of money which circulates in a kingdom. But an ability thus founded upon *paper*, is in the highest degree precarious, and dangerous. It may fail in one day, and prove the means of a shock that will dash us to pieces.

Our trade is diminished; and together with it, private circulation and credit. Our manufacturers are taken off to the navy and army. Depopulation goes on with rapidity. The cash of the nation is scraped together for public loans; and, little being left for any other purpose, Industry is cramped, Commerce starves, and Land falls. Many persons, foreseeing danger, begin to hoard the coin. The BANK begins to find that it has issued as much paper as it can support. Most of the new taxes have proved deficient. Complaints of distress are general. The spirits of men are soured, and many disposed to break out into open resistance. These evils will increase whilst the war continues: and whether we are invaded or not, must at last terminate in a dreadful convulsion.

CHAP.

CHAP. III.

Principles of the present Administration of Finance in France.

THE resources, œconomy, and character of the ministers of those states with which we are now contending, most unhappily for us admit of a very mortifying comparison with the measures and qualities of ministers of our own country. At the same time they most strongly enforce the necessity of the proposed reformation. What serious Englishman can read the language of the two last French edicts, and not tremble, when he maturely considers the different principles upon which that government and this are now proceeding, and the consequences which the respective systems, if persisted in, must inevitably produce to both nations.

The first of these edicts is given at Marly, October 17, 1779. " Louis, &c.
" Convinced that method and clearness in
" accounts are amongst the most proper
" means to preserve regulation and order in
" the

" the management of the finances, we have
" taken into confideration this important ob-
" ject; and we could not fee without regret
" that the ftatement of our revenues and of
" our expences was nothing more than the
" refult of fearch and fcattered intelligence
" collected together, and laid before us by
" the minifter of the finances, which made
" that knowledge, which is the moft inte-
" refting for the purpofe of forming our
" plans and our determinations, to depend
" upon the underftanding and accuracy of
" one fingle man. That the effential defect
" of this eftablifhment proceeded from hence,
" namely that the regiftry and accounts of
" our royal treafury, where the moft exact
" detail of the whole of our receipts and
" expences ought naturally to be found,
" furnifhed in thofe refpects only defective
" intelligence, and incomplete references:
" that one part of the impofts was neither
" carried into the treafury, nor even known
" of there, and that feveral forts of expences
" being by cuftom difcharged of different
" offices, neither did any trace of them
" exift in the royal treafury; yet neither
" could the documents of the chamber of

" accounts

" accounts supply the defects of this faulty
" arrangement; not only because all the pri-
" vate accounts are not brought in and au-
" dited till after the expiration of a very
" great number of years, but also because
" being dispersed amongst all the chambers
" of account in our kingdom, the general
" ballances and results thereof could not be
" formed without immoderate labour, and
" that this labour, slow and confused as such
" work always is, could never be of use.
" We have therefore been made sensible of
" what advantage it would be, as well to us
" as to our successors, to establish such a
" method of account as should transfer all
" receipts and payments to the royal treasu-
" ry, not indeed that they should always be
" transacted there in real specie, lest it should
" interrupt the facility of the public service
" or interfere with the management of par-
" ticular funds or appropriations; but at
" least that those accounts should be trans-
" ferred to the treasury in the manner of
" draughts and acquittance; so that, by
" opening the registry of the royal trea-
" sury, the exact ballance of the receipts
" and ordinary expences of each year, may
" be

" be clearly seen, and also in a separate ac-
" count the amount of the extraordinary
" expences and resources."

" We cannot but be aware that this
" method so useful and of such importance
" will render the state of our finances much
" less secret than it has hitherto been; and
" that we thereby contract an additional ob-
" ligation to keep up a constant correspond-
" ence between our revenues and our ordi-
" nary expences, because *that* alone is the
" foundation of credit and support of con-
" fidence; but we shall never desire any
" confidence but that which is just, and all
" other confidence we well know leads,
" sooner or later, to injustice and to breach
" of faith; from both of which we will
" ever preserve our reign; and we discover
" with satisfaction, that in pursuit of those
" views with which we are animated, the
" less we shall spread a veil over the state
" of our finances and their administration,
" the more claim we shall have to the love
" and confidence of our people."

The other edict is registered on the 3d of December 1779.

"Louis, &c.—Our people have been
"witnesses of the extensiveness of the
"force we have employed during the
"course of this year. We have not ef-
"fected this without very considerable ex-
"pences; but at the same time that we
"have procured extraordinary resources
"for that purpose, we have also augmented
"our revenue by *œconomy*, improvements,
"and *reformation* introduced into the
"department of our finances. And, ac-
"cording to the state of them which has
"been laid before us, we find that by vir-
"tue of these operations there subsists up
"to this moment an exact ballance be-
"tween our revenues, and our fixed and
"ordinary expences. And yet we have
"included in these expences all those an-
"nual payments which we continue punc-
"tually to make; though the arrets
"published under the late king would
"have authorized their suspension, from
"the commencement of a war and during
"the period of its continuance. This state

"of finance is certainly as satisfactory as the circumstances can well be supposed to admit; but it obliges us to find new aids to furnish the interest of those loans which the continuance of the war renders unavoidable."

Such language from the mouth of a French monarch, and such conduct in his Ministers, would at any time be circumstances of well founded alarm to this nation: in the present times, and contrasted with what we *hear* and *see* at home, they are serious beyond exaggeration (*a*).

To these considerations it may be proper briefly to subjoin the following facts.

(*a*) If the monarch has wisely come forward to his people, the people in their turn have advanced towards his ministers. And perhaps the most striking feature (and not the least alarming circumstance) in the French nation at this moment, is; that the haughty noble has foregone his idle claim of birth, and the vain native renounced his national prejudice and religious bigotry; and the whole nation with universal joy and satisfaction behold *Le Petit-fils d'un Horloger, un Huguenot* (to say every thing in one word) *un Genevois,* at the head of their finance, and a Monsieur Sartine, *fils d'un Marchand de Drap,* directing the operations of war,

The *whole* expence of the laſt war to France, was but little more than *half* the expence of it to this country. It was forty ſeven millions: which, as appears by the preceding chapter, is juſt what the preſent unnatural war has already coſt us up to Chriſtmas 1779.—The whole addition which that war made to their debt, was twenty ſix millions and a half: a conſiderable part of which time has ſince extinguiſhed.

The preſent war, being (on their part) almoſt entirely *naval*, will to them be much leſs coſtly.—At the end of 1778 the French miniſter had borrowed towards improving their marine, to the pitch at which we now ſee it, about five millions and a quarter ſterling: but had not impoſed any new taxes upon the people, the funds for paying the intereſt of the loans having been procured by ſavings in the revenue.— *Four millions* are expected to be their whole expence for the year 1779; which Mr. Neckar has already raiſed, and chiefly by life annuities: whilſt *twelve millions* extraordinary

traordinary will not be sufficient to satisfy our expences.

CHAP. IV

THE KING'S CIVIL LIST.

AT his present majesty's accession to the throne in the year 1760, the mode of appointing the private revenue of the crown, was, at his desire, altered; and instead of certain duties which used to be granted for the purpose of *supporting the civil government* with honour and dignity, a fixed and certain sum of eight hundred thousand pounds *per annum* was voted to him for life. Mr. Legge (at that time Chancellor of the Exchequer) in his Majesty's Name, gave to the House of Commons the most solemn and express assurances that his Majesty would strictly confine his expences to the ample provision then made for him by his people, and by him most thankfully and graciously
accepted

accepted. And his Majesty had himself from the throne on the 20th of November 1760, previously told them, that—" on "his part they might be assured of a re-"gular and becoming œconomy."

Notwithstanding these solemn assurances made to his people and the professions of *œconomy* with which he began his reign, in 1769, in consequence of an application made to them by the king, the House of Commons voted to his Majesty above *half a million* of money to discharge his debts. Upon the receipt of this enormous sum his Majesty on the 9th of May 1769, after returning to them his *particular thanks*, thus addresses the Commons— " Your readiness in relieving me from the " difficulties increasing upon me from the " continuance of that debt, I shall ever con- " sider as an additional motive for me to " endeavour to confine the expences of my " civil government within such bounds as " the honour of my crown can possibly " admit." (*a*)   In

---

(*a*) It is worth the reader's while to remark what a change of language, intentions, and subsequent conduct

In April 1777, application was a *second* time made by the minifter to the Commons for the payment of debts of the king to the amount of 618,340*l.* (*b*) And in the midft of the prefent expenfive war the firft lord of the Treafury had the modefty with the fame breath, to propofe an augmentation to his Majefty's *civil lift* of 100,000*l. per annum.*

It is not neceffary here to examine the feveral particulars of the account which was then laid before parliament : which, though fabricated to perplex and not to inform, and though unaccompanied with any voucher, yet was not able to mount up his Majefty's *open* and *avowable* expence any where near the increafed grant foli-

---

duct has been produced in his Majefty by the change of his counfellors and minifters. In 1760 the king's promife is abfolute.—" Strictly to confine his expences " to the ample provifion then made for him." In 1769 he will—"*endeavour to confine his expences within* " *fuch bounds as the honour of his crown* can poffibly " admit."

(*b*) Thefe repeated applications and debts unaccounted for, might perhaps without any impropriety be ftiled—The *extraordinaries* of the king's *civil lift.*

solicited and obtained from the *honest* trustees of the people.

When the speaker at the bar of the House of Lords presented the *civil list* bill to his Majesty, he addressed him in the following words;

"By this bill, Sir, and the respectful
"circumstances which preceded and ac-
"companied it, your Commons have given
"the fullest and clearest proof of their
"zeal and affection for your Majesty. For,
"*in a time of public distress, full of difficulty*
"and *danger*, their constituents labouring
"under *burthens almost too heavy to be*
"*borne*, your faithful Commons post-
"poned all other business, and with as
"much dispatch as the nature of their
"proceedings would admit, have not only
"granted to your Majesty a *large present*
"*supply*, but also a *very great* additional
"revenue: great *beyond example*: great,
"beyond your Majesty's HIGHEST EX-
"PENCE.—But all this, Sir, they have
"done in *well grounded confidence* that
"you

"you will *apply wisely* what they have granted liberally."

How *well grounded* the confidence of the Commons, and how *wise* the application of the King, can only be determined when that application shall have been clearly developed by time, which brings to light the hidden things of darkness; and when (besides the loss of our colonies in America and the establishment of despotism in Canada) all the other approaching consequences of the *obsequiousness* of parliament shall have demonstrated the *wisdom* of such application.

In the mean time we will content ourselves for the present with laying before the public the few following notorious facts, under this article of expenditure.

Ministers to foreign Courts.

At a time when Great Britain was at the head of the most powerful alliance that ever was formed in Europe, the article of *foreign ministers* appears to have cost our glorious King William, a sum amounting *per annum* to nearly — — £.45,000

The King's Civil List.

	l.
This fame article in the laft moſt glorious war amounted to no more *per annum* than	50,000
Whilſt in the latter years of his preſent Majeſty's reign it has been found to amount to no leſs than	98,000

And yet, with all our augmented embaſſies, we are ſtill to learn whether we have a ſingle ally to ſecond us in this our hour of diſtreſs; or whether we have ſo much as cultivated the friendſhip or obtained even the good wiſhes of any one power in Europe.

Secret ſervice Money.

	l.
This article which coſt *per annum* to our late honeſt ſovereign King George the Second, in his laſt juſt, and therefore glorious war	44,000
Was in 1777 increaſed *per ann.* to	86,000

Let our admirals and generals be called upon to declare the advantageous difference between

between the *intelligence* now received, and that which was received laſt war; and how far that difference has contributed to the numerous diſgraces we have already in the preſent war undergone.

Penſions avowedly paid out of the King's Civil Liſt.

	l.
Theſe in the late king's reign amounted *per annum* to	68,300
At preſent they amount *per ann.* to	127,000
So that the expence at preſent upon theſe three articles alone is yearly	311,000

And the increaſed profuſion in the preſent reign in theſe articles only beyond that of the late reign amounts *per annum* to — 149,000

Thus have his Majeſty's moſt ſolemn and repeated aſſurances of oeconomy been fulfilled. Thus have the yearly aggravated and accumulating burthens of his *diminiſhed* and impoveriſhed ſubjects been conſulted! Subjects ſo impoveriſhed by the profecution of this inhuman and unnatural war; that if the private loffes fuftained by individuals were collected and ftated together in one aggregate fum they would make the national expences, enormous as they are, lofe their enormity in the comparifon.

CHAP. V.

EXTRAORDINARIES OF THE ARMY.

(Lord North's Civil Lift.)

SECT. I.

Comparifon of the prefent extraordinaries with thofe of former wars.

IT is the ufage of parliament to call for the eftimates of the different military eftablifhments to be laid before them at the beginning of every feffion.

The eftimates of the army are,

1ft. The guards and garrifons; which were formerly called the home guard.

2dly,

2dly, The forces for the plantations; this head contains thofe for North America, the Weft Indies, Gibraltar, Minorca, and Africa.

3dly, The foreign forces in Britifh pay. This is only in time of war.

Thefe three eftimates ftate the full pay of the officers as well as that of the private men (clothing included) in every regiment. There is alfo an eftimate of the charge for general and general ftaff officers.

In the firft of thefe eftimates there is an allowance of 32,000*l*. for the expence of *garrifons at home*.

In the fecond eftimate there is a charge for the *garrifons abroad*, and *officers* ferving in them; befides a charge of *provifions* for the *forces ferving abroad*, which is indeed inadequate to the *prefent* expences in that article. Thefe two eftimates contain alfo an allowance of 24,000*l*. for contingencies (i. e. 20,000*l*. in the firft eftimate for *guards and garrifons*; and 4000*l*. in the

the second estimate for the plantations); which sum it must also be confessed, is only a feeble anticipation of the *present* incidental charges: but it proves however the parliamentary principle as well as the practice of limiting by parliament itself both military extraordinaries and contingencies.

Certain expences beyond these parliamentary allowances for extraordinaries and contingencies, form the *present list of extraordinaries*. And the accounts of such extraordinaries are according to exigencies laid before parliament once or oftener in each session; accompanied however with this most unconstitutional circumstance, that nothing is left to the discretion of parliament——For the debt is not only incurred, but paid——Incurred with the minister's approbation, and paid by his orders only. (*a*)

The

(*a*) This payment in the first instance by the minister's order, must be made out of money voted before by parliament and appropriated by them to other purposes:

Extraordinaries of the Army.

The following account, taken with as much care as poſſible from the journals of parliament will ſhew the *alarming growth* of this abuſe.

The extraordinaries in King William's war, were   £. 1,200,000

This war laſted about *nine* years: the expence therefore of each year's extraordinaries of King William's war, was upon an average about 133,000*l.* which is about *two* pounds *ſeven* ſhillings *per ann.* for each man in the army.

The extraordinaries in Queen Ann's war, were   £.2,000,000

This

---

poſes: a conduct which in better times has been reprobated and very juſtly condemned by the reſolutions of parliament.

Beſides that, by this method the miniſter is enabled to deceive the public; by throwing back for a time the great expence of the war, and concealing the magnitude and extent of the national engagements.

This war lasted about *eleven* years: the extraordinaries therefore of this war amounted each year, upon an average, to about 180,000*l. per ann.* The calculations *per man* cannot be made in this war, on account of the difficulty of finding the numbers voted; because they were sometimes an indefinite proportion of foreign troops; and sometimes a large sum was voted for a particular part of the war, generally, and on account.

The extraordinaries in George the Second's first war, were - - £.3,500,000

This war lasted about *nine* years; the extraordinaries therefore amounted to something under 400,000*l. per annum.* Which is about *five* pounds *per annum* for each man in the army. (*a*)

Con-

(*a*) To avoid puzzling the reader, we have hitherto given only gross sums, with a constant leaning however to the higher sum.

Comparison of the *extraordinaries* of the *four* first years of the *last* war, with the *four* first years of the *present* war.

Last War.		*Present War.*	
In 1755	£. 504,977	In 1775	£. 845,165
1756	697,547	1776	2,170,602
1757	1,232,369	1777	2,200,223
1758	1,166,785	1778	3,026,137
Total	3,601,678	Total	8,242,127

Number of men voted in these four years 347,223	Number of men voted in these four years 314,918
Therefore at an average 10l. 7s. 6d. for *extraordinaries* for each man *per annum*.	Therefore at an average 26l. 1s. 6d. for *extraordinaries* for each man *per annum*.

N. B. We have proceeded no farther in our comparison of the *extraordinaries* of these two wars, because the extraordinaries for 1779 will not be laid before parliament till the year 1780, after the present recess.

It should be observed that in 1778 the Militia was embodied, and three regiments of fencible men were raised in North Britain: the total of both is 39,206 men, which are not included in the above account

count becaufe the former were embodied only in the middle of the year, and both thefe corps (as well as many other augmentations made in that year) were at home and caufed but very little extraordinary expence.

The following comparative view of extraordinaries will not be unworthy of the reader's attention:

Extraordinaries of King William's war of nine years	£. 1,200,000
Extraordinaries of Queen Anne's war of eleven years	2,000,000
Total of thefe two wars of twenty years	3,200,000
Extraordinaries of *laft year* only	3,026,137
Difference	173,863

Thus we fee that the extraordinaries of 1778 (voted by Parliament in 1779) are but 173,863*l.* fhort of the extraordinaries for the *whole* of two great wars (which lafted twenty years).

Extraordinaries of the Army. 43

We may also consider that the WHOLE SUPPLY for the first year of Queen Anne's war (with 40,000 seamen included) was but 3,535,457*l.* which is only 509,320*l.* more than the bare *extraordinaries of the army* for the year 1778.

The *excess* of the extraordinaries for the four first years of the present war, is 4,640,449*l.* more than the extraordinaries of the four first years of the last war.

And the extraordinaries for *four* years only of the present war amount to *one million and an half sterling*, more than all the extraordinaries of King William's, Queen Anne's, and George the Second's first war together, which wars comprize the space of *twenty-nine* years.

It must be observed for the sake of precision, that through the whole of this chapter we have not confined ourselves to the extraordinaries (properly so called) which are laid before Parliament under that title; but we have added to those accounts such parts of the votes of credit as have been stated to be applied to the extraordinary services of the Army.

SECT. II.

Sums remitted to North America, of which no Account has been given to Parliament.

IN 1775	—	£. 408,809
1776	—	799,973
1777	—	1,052,060
1778	—	1,535,701 *(a)*

Total 3,796,543

The accounts of the sums remitted in 1779 have not yet been presented to parliament: therefore the remittances of that year are not yet known; but they will probably exceed those of 1778.

Besides these sums, the pay of the army is also remitted to North America by Messrs. Harley and Drummond.—The remit-

---

(a) The public will undoubtedly learn with astonishment, that this *million and a half* sterling, is a charge of *some kind or other* for the army, over and above *Pay* and *Clothing*, *Provisions* and *Freight*, *Transport Service at large*, *Ordnance*, *Expence* of *Indians*, *Rum*, *Hospitals*, *Pay* of *General* and *Staff Officers*, Camp Equipage, and all the various other *known* allowances to the army. And yet of this *million and a half* sterling, Parliament has not had any account whatever.

remittances are sometimes made in Spanish or Portugal coins, and sometimes in English coin: the quantity of the latter exported is said to have alarmed the Bank of England *(a)*.

SECT.

(*a*) The motives for making what is called the *gold contract*, as well as the contract itself, do well deserve a thorough investigation; in which the *covenants* and the *non-performance* of those covenants ought not to be passed over.

The by-operations of this contract may be judged of by the following well authenticated fact.

The agents for the contractors in Canada having collected a good deal of money by disposing of bills on the Treasury at low prices, made use of it in monopolizing the corn of the province. In executing this design they doubled and nearly tripled the price of corn, and produced the danger of a famine in some parts of the province. But complaints having been made, and the governor having shewn great resentment, they were displaced; and new agents were appointed, who took with them to Quebec from hence a large sum in specie, which rendering bills unnecessary, raised them to their former value.

It is likewise well known that the agents, in sending rations to garrisons in the interior parts of the province, have sometimes sent rations for *thousands*, when perhaps the garrison has consisted only of a few *hundreds*; the surplus being intended to be distributed amongst the Indians in order to conciliate and keep them quiet.

SECT. III.

Contracts and the Mode of them.

TO examine into the mode of making all public contracts, or to state *all* the obvious objections to those made by the present ministers, requires more time and space than is allotted to this part of the present publication.

There was much complaint on the subject of contracts during the last war. Various motions were made and inquiries were *commenced* in Parliament. Since the peace all mankind have been shocked at the enormous fortunes made by contractors, which could not have been accumulated without the most flagrant impositions on the public.

Notwithstanding which the present Treasury, instead of profiting by the experience of the last war (though Lord North had a place at that Board all the time) has set out in this unnatural war with a design not

not to check the public expenditure, but to increase the *Influence* of the *Crown* by the most unexampled extension of profusion, dissipation, and bad œconomy.

The following fact, it is presumed, will be sufficient to justify this charge to its utmost extent.

In the last war the contract for supplying the troops with fresh and salt provisions was made with Sir William Baker; who had carried on a trade with North America for a long course of years, and whose dealings upon that continent as well as his character in all other respects naturally pointed him out as the fittest and most capable person to execute the contract. The contract was made with him at *six pence* per ration, to be delivered into the king's stores in North America. Various conditions were annexed; and amongst others, that he should have a partner who should be always resident there on the spot, and should correspond with him and occasionally with government. And this contract was accordingly executed to the satisfaction

tisfaction of the government and the army.

The prefent Treafury, inftead of either following that mode (or correcting it if experience had proved correction neceffary) began by extending the contract and dividing it amongft a number of perfons, unconnected with each other, and in no way belonging to that particular trade, or intitled by any particular knowledge of or dealings in North America.——(*a*) Inftead of delivering in the provifions to the king's ftores in *North America*, the Treafury agrees with thefe gentlemen to deliver them into the king's ftorehoufes at *Corke*.—To hide the exorbitance of the contract, the Treafury fixes the price of each ration to be 5½*d*. which is indeed in appearance

---

(*a*) *Contractors.*

Mr. Burfoot, treafurer of Chrift's Hofpital, a contractor for rum.

Mr. Harley, a *wine* merchant, contractor for *remittances, provifions,* and *clothing.*

Sometimes the clerks of the rum contractors are ftated as partners.

The chairman of the Eaft-India company, the deputy chairman of the Eaft-India company, &c.

appearance at the rate of one farthing *per ration* less than the contract with Sir William Baker. But in this latter contract, government is to be at the expence of transporting those provisions, and of arming and convoying those transports from Corke to North America, together with all risques and the additional expence of storehouses in North America. All which additional charges may be reasonably estimated, so as to make the ration, when delivered, cost to the public upwards of *ten* pence.—That the public may judge of some of these expences, it is necessary to inform them that the draughts alone of the Commissary at Corke (Mr. Gordon) amount in three years only, to 39,906*l*.

SECT IV.

Rum Contract.

IN the month of September 1775, Lord North thought it necessary to send to the British army (then besieged in Boston by an American militia) various supplies of *comfort* to be distributed as rations to the troops besides their regular rations of ordinary provisions. Mr. Atkinson (partner of Messrs. Mure and Son, *West-India* merchants) was introduced to Lord North, by Mr. Robinson, the Secretary of the Treasury, as a fit person to undertake this business. All the articles were to be executed by commission, except the article of RUM; the necessity of sending which, for any thing that appears, may have been suggested to Lord North by the contractor (Atkinson) himself: as very little of that article had been used in the last war, and then only upon extraordinary occasions; and from the commencement of the American troubles to that time, no direct requi-

requisition had been made by the Generals in North America for RUM.

Lord North however (by what motives induced or upon what consultation held, is neither known nor necessary to be known) determined to send them *Rum:* and preferring a specific agreement to any allowance of commission upon this head, because the latter might—(at such a distance as the West Indies!) raise the price here upon the public, Mr. Atkinson proposed to supply the Rum *in Jamaica* at the price which the Victualling Office paid for the supply of the fleet upon that station, be it what it might: and that he would afterwards engage to carry it to North America at a very high stated charge for freight, insurance, leakage, &c. which high charge he modestly called the *usual* allowance for those articles. The quantity of Rum proposed was 100,000 gallons. This agreement was merely *verbal*, it was never reduced to writing, it was made by Lord North *alone*, and does not appear to have been

been communicated to the Board of Treasury after their summer recess. *(a)*

(b) The *Secretary* of the Victualling Office (who died soon after) being applied to by the Treasury for the price paid by that Board for Rum *in Jamaica*) is said to have answered *simply* that their agreement was for four shillings and four-pence per gallon; without acquainting the Treasury that the custom of the Victualling Office was to receive tenders of contracts in which almost all the different species of provisions are rated far *under* their real value, and the *compensation* to the contractor arises from the extraordinary high price allowed for Rum.

Upon

(*a*) However incredible it may appear, yet it is a certain fact, that the Treasury never knew that *Rum* was regularly distributed as part of the soldiers rations, till the end of the year 1777, although they had made one contract in 1775 for 100,000 gallons of Rum, and another in 1776 for 500,000 gallons.

(*b*) It does not appear that the Victualing Board itself was ever applied to.

Rum Contract: 53

Upon this fact thus stated was Lord North's agreement for *Rum* founded. *(a)* No farther inquiry upon that head was made at the Victualling Office for near two years.

No urgent and pressing necessity for a supply of Rum could be pleaded in excuse for this exorbitancy of the price; because the Rum thus agreed for in September 1775, was not to be delivered till the ensuing campaign of 1776. Eight or nine months were to elapse between the bargain and the time of delivery.

Neither can any pretence of ignorance be reasonably admitted: for the Capital swarmed with West India merchants and planters, who could have informed the Treasury

---

(a) Besides that the price given by the Victualling Office for Rum is always connected with other articles, it is stipulated in the Victualling Office contract that the Rum shall be *six months old*; a circumstance which adds much to its value, and of which Mr. Atkinson (before the Rum-Committee in 1778) declared himself ignorant.

Treasury of the little variation of the price of Rum for years past in the island of Jamaica, *(a)* and of the enormity of the price proposed. But none of these were consulted. If the Etiquette of the public Boards had absurdly confined them to communicate only with each other; yet, even in that case, the Treasury Board might have learned from the Victualling Office, that at the very time when Lord North was agreeing with Mr. Atkinson for Rum to be delivered in *Jamaica* at 4*s*. 4*d*. per gallon, that Board was buying *Jamaica* Rum for the Navy here in London, at the mast-head, at 2*s*. 2*d*. per gallon. *(b)* This is, at the first view, *half the price* given to Mr. Atkinson: but the owner of the Rum sold here had been at the charge of freight, insurance, leakage, commission, &c. to bring the Rum to England: from all which articles

---

(a) In the spring of each year 2*s*. and 6*d*. currency per gallon, which is about 1*s*. and 9*d*. halfpenny sterling, is reckoned rather a high price.

(b) This appeared by the accounts of the Victualling Office, laid before the Rum Committee in the House of Commons.

ticles of expence Mr. Atkinson's Rum deliverable in *Jamaica* was totally free.

In the beginning of the year 1776 Lord North made another contract for 500,000 gallons of Jamaica Rum; the greatest part of which was to be furnished by the same Mr. Atkinson. The Treasury taking the former *moderate* price of 4*s*. 4*d*. as a *datum* not to be exceeded, made this contract at the specific price of 5*s*. 3*d*. per gallon, to be delivered in North America. This price of 5*s*. 3*d*. is very near the former agreement, if you add to the 4*s*. 4*d*. *in Jamaica*, only reasonable and probable charges for freight, insurance, leakage, &c. from Jamaica to *North America*.

This *datum* of 4*s*. 4*d*. per gallon (said Mr. Secretary Robinson before the committee) was taken by the Treasury, they not knowing that any objection was made to that price till a considerable time afterwards; that is, till the month of May 1777: unfortunately indeed, about that time, or rather before the Easter recess, the slumber (or more truly perhaps the confident

fident security) of the Treasury was interrupted by some pointed questions concerning the *extraordinaries:* and particularly concerning the article of *Rum*; which, though less considerable in size than many other articles, yet as to exorbitance of price, stood in high relief above the rest.—The Treasurer at these questions awaked; was at first peevish; then confounded; asked for information from right and left; received it; and was only the more confused by the communication; did not know the difference between *currency* and *sterling* (a mere trifle of 40 per cent); and being astonished at the *nakedness* of his own profusion—he thinks—but he really does not know—he believes—his friends tell him—but he can't be positive—that the price he agreed to give must be *currency*.

After the Easter recess, Lord North comes to Parliament armed now with facts, calculations and confidence. His 4*s.* 4*d.* he now acknowledges to be *sterling:* he is proud to avow it, the contract could not be executed more cheaply. His calcu-

calculations are exact; and he proves by papers in his hand, that every gallon of Rum carried from Jamaica to North America, by Messrs. Mure and Atkinson, stood them in 5s. 11d; if not in six shillings per gallon.

Those who had blamed this contract were confounded at the hardiness of these assertions; and no wonder. The man who had been suspected of making an overreaching or scandalous contract with the Board of Treasury, is, after a strict examination, proved by the first lord of that board (whose character was involved in the transaction) to have been a loser of 12 per cent. by his bargain.

This *extraordinary* calculation was however but short-lived, and another was afterwards produced of a more probable kind; which supposed the contractor to have had some (but those not unreasonable) profits. These two last calculations were only delivered in loose parliamentary conversations,¹ and were afterwards most clearly and compleatly overthrown by inconteſtable evidence

evidence, before a Committee of the House of Commons appointed in the beginning of the year 1778 for the purpose of examination: and from the *report of that committee* all the material facts contained in this section have been taken.

But, to return——Mr. Atkinson being alarmed at the approaches towards detection which had been made by conversation in Parliament in spring 1777; requested that the Lords of the Treasury would refer his *second* contract to the consideration of some West India merchants, for them to report their opinion upon it: * Mr. Atkinson adding, that if those merchants would declare that the contract might at the time of making it have been undertaken, or could now be *reasonably* undertaken upon lower terms, he would wave the benefit of this *second* contract and accept of such lower price as they may report to be *reasonable* for *a contractor* to receive.

Men

---

* It is well worthy of observation, that neither Mr. Atkinson nor the Treasury had ever the confidence to propose referring the *first* Rum Contract.

Men of high character in the mercantile world, and particularly in the West India trade, *(a)* accepted of this disagreeable office. Their report very judiciously carries in it no distinct or decided *declaration* upon the *reasonableness* or *unreasonableness* of the *contract:* they studiously avoid it: but they give a calculation of the *first* cost of the Rum, including casks, island leakage, commission and shipping charges at Jamaica, which amount to *two* shillings and *five* pence *sterling* per gallon. And they make the Rum when delivered in *North America*, stand the contractor in about *four* shillings and *one* farthing *sterling* per gallon.

Taking this report as it stands thus *nakedly*, and without explanation, Mr. Atkinson stated his profit on the contract to be only $22\tfrac{1}{2}$ per cent.—But when the merchants to whom the reference had been made, came to be examined before the committee — (for whatever might have been Mr. Atkinson's views and hopes by this proposal of his to refer the contract to merchants,

---

(a) Messrs. Long, Neave, and Creighton.

merchants, he did not by it escape the examination by a Committee of the House of Commons)—it plainly appeared by their evidence, that they had *already* in their report, by which they made the price of the Rum, when delivered in North America, amount to *four* shillings and one farthing, they had already calculated all the different charges in such a manner as (to use their own expression) *to leave a profit in the belly of each.*

It is a circumstance much to the honour of these gentlemen, that they have in their report, laid down with great decency this strong and useful maxim——" that *private* contracts are most liable to exceptions."

Mr. Atkinson, not satisfied with this report, persuaded the treasury to make a new reference, upon *some parts* of the former, to the same merchants. The answer of these gentlemen shews a proper resentment of such treatment, and deserves the reader's attention.—They state, that they had in their report made the *most ample* allowance for every charge which *even in these*

these perilous times (m) could have affected the undertaking. But whether the *contractor's* profits have been less or greater than *his expectations*, they said, was a subject of investigation which they did not think proper to go into. They declared that they had made their estimates upon the *most liberal* principles: but that they were not proper judges, what allowances should be made to *contractors*.

The *Rum Committee* had likewise before them a *third* contract made with Mr. Atkinson by Sir William Howe. The price was not fixed and the payments seemed (at least at that time) to be suspended on account of the report of the merchants and of the doubts thrown upon the propriety of the *second* contract. It is however to be observed that this *third* contract was

---

(*m*) N. B. This allowance was made by them in the summer 1778.

The captures of our ships by the Americans did not commence till about August 1776; which was after the proper time for the delivery of the Rum agreed for in the two first contracts.

was attended with a very confiderable collateral advantage: for, to prevent (as was faid) the American rebels from being fupplied with Weft India Rum, orders were fent to the Weft India Governours to grant *licences* for the exportation of Rum, Molaffes, &c. *to the contractors only.* The merchants and planters here at home remonftrated upon the fubject, and thefe orders were indeed afterwards countermanded: but as long as it fubfifted, the contractors had an abfolute *monopoly* of thofe articles, not only for the *army*, but alfo for the fupply of the *great towns* in which the Army might be quartered.—The wifh for a monopoly of fupplying even the *rebels too* cannot with any colour be fufpected; the confcience of contractors and the cleannefs of *their* hands in matter of gain, making them no doubt lefs liable to fufpicion than any other mercenary exporters.

It may not perhaps be impertinent here, to take fome little notice of the *Committee* which was appointed by the *Majority* of the Houfe of Commons, to examine into thefe contracts. It confifted of 21 members:
of

of whom 15 were perfons who almoft always voted with the Minifters: viz.—The prefent Secretary of War, The Counfel to the Board of Ordnance, The Cofferer of the Houfhold, The Treafurer of the Navy, many ftrong perfonal friends of Lord North, &c. &c.

At the outfet of the inquiry Mr. Jenkinfon propofed, that Mr. Atkinfon fhould be firft examined. This was however given up, upon its being infifted that the *Servants of the Crown* were the perfons who ought to be examined concerning the expenditure of public money, and not the Contractors. Mr. Atkinfon was however fo far mafter of the proceedings of the Committee, that after the evidence had been clofed and the plan for the report laid down and in great meafure approved; yet the inquiry was again opened in order to receive a moft *extraordinary* paper (not to fpeak more harfhly of it) from Mr. Atkinfon, which he had procured to be figned by a great number of *underwriters*, to fhew the difficulty if not impoffibility of getting infurance made upon fhip or fhips.

'This led the committee into a new line of evidence, the refult of which deftroyed the tendency of that paper, and turned out to the confufion of Mr. Atkinfon and of his friends in the Committee.

The Contractor was at laft, however reluctantly, given up in the Committee: though it is worthy the remark of the Public, that his progrefs in *treafury favour* has been in proportion to their difcovery of the demerits of his contracts: (*a*) for

---

(*a*) When this contract for Rum was alluded to in the Houfe of Lords, on the 15th of December 1779, The Lord Chancellor, in anfwer to the allufion, obferved—" that whatever proofs on this fubject might or might not have been given before a Committee of the Houfe of Commons, there were certainly, at that time, neither proofs nor charge before the Houfe of Lords; and that confequently the allegation would at that time make no impreffion upon his mind. But fo far he would be free to fay in regard to the complaint made by fome noble lords of *hard names* being applied to that alledged tranfaction; that if it fhould ever appear to be true, that any Minifter of this Country had made a Contract out of meafure beyond the proper and ordinary price of the article contracted for, and which article for public fervice he might have been fupplied with on much inferior terms; that this overcharge fhould be proved and appear

Rum Contract.

In 1775 he received of public money — 108,000
In 1776 ——— ——— about 400,000
In 1777 ——— ——— about 600,000
In 1778 ——— ——— about 672,000

£. 1,780,000

N. B. To this muſt be added the ſums paid to him in 1779, which have not yet appeared (*a*).

Before we cloſe this ſection, it may be proper to inform the reader, that the committee in the courſe of its proceedings diſcovered great abuſes and ſhameful miſmanagement in the Victualling board; particularly in their method of making their contracts.——The committee diſcovered

pear plainly to have been the fact; and if, after ſuch proof made known, the miniſter ſhould notwithſtanding continue to contract with and employ for the public ſervice the ſame unconſcionable contractor: that then, in ſuch a caſe, according to his (the Chancellor's) opinion, no *names* whatever could poſſibly be *too hard* to apply to ſuch a conduct.

(*a*) Will it be credited, that after all theſe proceedings concerning the *Rum* contracts; after all the foreneſs and diſgrace of the miniſter upon this ſubject; a *new office* has lately been created, ſufficiently lucrative to inſure the acceptance of a field officer; under the ſtile and title of RUM TASTER to the Army!

covered also that the conduct of the Treasury was (at least) marked with ignorance, imbecility, and neglect.—— That the references of accounts to the comptroller of the army were a mere mockery. That the business of that office (instead of control) was solely to examine vouchers. And that money was sometimes reported as fit to be paid to the contractors; although the contractors had not produced the necessary documents prescribed by the terms of their contracts to intitle them to such payment.

SECT. V.

Bills drawn by Governours.

BEFORE the year 1755, there was scarcely such an article to be found in the journals of parliament as *bills* drawn by *governours*.

The following is an account of governours bills, from 1755 to 1778, extracted from the journals of the House of Commons

mons, as correctly as the nature of the subject and the manner of making up the accounts of extraordinaries will permit.

In 1755	— £.	850
1756	—	1,969
1757	—	6,705
1758	—	4,130
1759	—	6,769
1760	—	13,782
1761	—	4,631
1762	—	0,000
1763	—	0,000
1764	—	8,754
1765	—	37,390
1766	—	52,332
1767	—	28,506
1768	—	26,625
1769	—	18,420
1770	—	20,066
1771	—	30,017
1772	—	22,166
1773	—	60,144
1774	—	37,995
1775	—	17,241
1776	—	90,909
1777	—	91,247
1778	—	94,490

The average annual amount of governours bills, from 1765 (which was the firſt year after the war) to 1775, both years incluſive, is leſs *per ann.* than 32,000l.

Since 1775, almoſt every governour, both in North America and the Weſt Indies, ſeems to have had a ſingular reliſh for this kind of correſpondence with the Treaſury, and ſeduloufly to have followed up its practice. This appears by obſerving that the average annual amount of the three laſt years, 1776, 1777, and 1778, is more *per ann.* than 92,000l. That is nearly *triple* the ſum of the annual average amount of the former years.

We muſt obſerve, that moſt of theſe draughts came from the Weſt India iſlands, which, ſo far from ſtanding in need of any particular parliamentary or royal-money-aſſiſtance, were capable of contributing materially, and did contribute to the general ſupport of the empire.— This is clearly proved by the plan laid down and executed in 1763, and in the following years, for ſelling the lands to the

the firſt ſettlers, which poured a conſiderable ſum into the public Treaſury. And it is well known that the 4½ per cent. tax was not refuſed in the ceded iſlands upon any allegation of inability to pay it; but on account of the illegal and unconſtitutional exertion of prerogative authority by which it was levied (*a*).

The reader may perhaps imagine, that in theſe laſt three years of hoſtilities and apprehended attacks, the ſums drawn for by the governours may have been expended in putting Dominica, St. Vincent's, Grenada, Virginia, and the other governments on the continent into a proper ſtate of defence; but it is neceſſary to acquaint him, that the *engineers, cannon, ammunition, ſmall arms, ſtores, fortifications, &c.* for thoſe places (to an amazing amount) are voted by parliament in the *ordnance* eſtimate.——With what additional indignation

---

(*a*) The conſtitutional reader will find the doctrine of Lord Mansfield, in the Court of King's-Bench, upon this ſubject, very ably ſtated and anſwered in Mr. Baron Maſeres's *Canadian Freeholder.* Vol. II.

nation and shame will the English reader farther reflect, that either the standard of France, or the standard of America is now flying in each of those plantations, from whence those enormous draughts upon the Treasury were made.

Omitting a variety of smaller bills drawn from North and South Carolina, Virginia, New York, &c. we have selected the following remarkable bills drawn in 1776, 1777, and 1778.

Governour of *Tobago* (in *one* year) —— —— £. 19,017
Governour of Virginia (in *one* year) —— —— 25,000
Governour of *East Florida* (in two years) —— —— 20,135
Governour of *Grenada* (in two years) —— —— 21,750
Governour of Dominica (in *two* years) —— —— 24,812
Governour of St. Vincent's (in two years) —— —— 26,993

It must be observed that the *last* of these articles is the *only one* which the minister has

has condefcended to explain to parliament, and that explanation deferves to be *recorded*.

Lord North faid, that the governour of St. Vincent's had, of his own authority, created a Caraib war, and had incurred by that meafure, much heavier expences than thofe ftated to be incurred by him in the extraordinaries of the army; and that he (Lord North) had ordered *other* bills to a confiderable amount to be protefted (*a*).

This governour was fuffered to continue in his government till the French had conquered the ifland; which conqueft, it ought to be obferved, was effected by a French force *inferior* to that of the Englifh garrifon.

N. B.

(*a*) The noble lord, when he difapproved the expence, did not drop a word of blame upon the governour, for the *injuftice* and *cruelty* of fuch a war. Although his lordfhip muft very well know that the inhumanity of *his own* former war againft the Caraibs, as well as that of the governour's latter war againft thofe unhappy Savages, was that which threw them into the arms of our enemy and caufed them to unite againft us with the French invaders.

N. B. It is two years ago since the *assembly* of St. Vincent's made representations against their governour's conduct; and charged him with facts of so scandalous a nature, and so shocking to humanity, that we shall forbear to mention them until they are either legally proved, or smothered by ministerial authority.——These matters were alluded to by a right honourable member in the House of Commons. The Minister took up the governour's cause and was pleased to distinguish him by the honourable appellation of his "*friend.*" This appellation produced its natural effect upon an *intelligent* majority.——When these representations of the *assembly* were laid before the American secretary, he also was pleased to procrastinate all examination.

Had the assembly been attended to in due time, Lord North's *friend* might not perhaps have drawn upon the Treasury to such an amount as to oblige his lordship *at last* to protest his *friend*'s bills: and St. Vincent's might not perhaps have surrendered with a garrison superior to the *French* force that attacked it.

CHAP.

AN ODE

IN IMITATION OF

ALCÆUS.

Οὐ λίθοι ὀδὲ ξύλα, ὀδὲ
Τέχνη τεκτόνων αἱ πόλεις εἰσὶν,
Ἀλλ' ὅπου ποτ' ἂν ὦσιν ΑΝΔΡΕΣ
Αὑτοὺς σώζειν εἰδότες,
Ἐνταῦθα τείχη καὶ πόλεις.

ALC. quoted by ARISTIDES.

WHAT constitutes a State?
Not high-rais'd battlement or labour'd mound,
   Thick wall or moated gate;
Not cities proud with spires and turrets crown'd;
   Not bays and broad-arm'd ports,
Where, laughing at the storm, rich navies ride,
   Not starr'd and spangled courts,
Where low-brow'd baseness wafts perfume to pride,

No:—MEN, high-minded MEN,
With pow'rs as far above dull brutes endued
In forest, brake, or den,
As beasts excel cold rocks and brambles rude;
Men, who their *duties* know,
But know their *rights*, and, knowing, dare maintain,
Prevent the long-aim'd blow,
And crush the tyrant while they rend the chain:
These constitute a State,
And sov'reign LAW, *that state's collected will*,
O'er thrones and globes elate
Sits Empress, crowning good, repressing ill;
Smit by her sacred frown
The fiend *Discretion* like a vapour sinks,
And e'en the all-dazzling *Crown*
Hides his faint rays, and at her bidding shrinks.
Such *was* this heav'n-lov'd isle,
Than *Lesbos* fairer and the *Cretan* shore!
No more shall freedom smile?
Shall *Britons* languish, and be MEN no more?
Since all must life resign,
Those sweet rewards, which decorate the brave,
'Tis folly to decline,
And steal inglorious to the silent grave.

PRINTED AND DISTRIBUTED GRATIS BY THE SOCIETY
FOR CONSTITUTIONAL INFORMATION.

SECT VI.

Extraordinary Appointments and Contingent Bills.

THE abuse of creating *new* and *unnecessary* offices in the army, has already made most shameful advances, and is accelerating in its progress.

The abuse of allowing *Contingent Bills,* though hitherto not so considerable in point of expence, is a quick growing and dangerous evil: its advances will not be less rapid, because it is of a more underhand and secret nature than appointments.

Formerly new appointments were dealt out with a very sparing hand, and *Contingent Bills* were almost unknown, or at least inconsiderable, even in the accounts of *principals* in certain offices; such as those of the Quarter Master General and Adjutant General. But in the course of the present war, even the *deputies* and *assistants* to those officers, besides many others of inferior

ferior defcription, have affumed a right to *contingencies*. Such rights are not only eafily admitted, but feem to be encouraged by the minifter; and parliament is now become too complaifant to call the propriety of them in queftion.

The few following inftances of thefe abufes are felected out of the extraordinaries of the American war, only as a flight fpecimen for the reader's perufal.

1ft. In 1775 a commiffary was appointed at *five pounds per day* to mufter the German troops then taken and propofed to be taken into his Majefty's fervice. There was fome pretence for an appointment of this fort in the clofe of that year and in the beginning of 1776: becaufe the king's engagements with the German princes were then become very extenfive; and an officer of rank in that commiffion might be ufeful to prevent, or to correct abufes in muftering. But in the following years, the additional troops hired in Germany, as well as the annual recruits from thence for their corps in North America, were too incon-

inconsiderable to require an inspection of this costly sort, and were besides open to checks of a less expensive nature. Yet the same commissary has been continued ever since at *five pounds per day.*—He is also at the same time a general officer upon the staff in England.—He has besides been paid *contingencies* as *deputy* Adjutant General, in the extraordinaries of each of the four last years.——And in his capacity of *Commissary* above *sixty thousand* pounds of public money appear to have passed through his hands, without any account or explanation whatever given to parliament.

Unless it can be called a parliamentary account or explanation, that Lord North did indeed condescend to tell the House of Commons, in a mere conversation upon this subject—that he *supposed* the money might perhaps be applied to pay some *contingencies* of the foreign troops in their march to the place of embarkation.

2d. Another officer appears in the extraordinaries to be appointed for the same purpose as the foregoing, at *three pounds per*

per day. And this gentleman alſo charges contingent expences.

3d. So vigilant has the Miniſter been in this article of muſtering foreign troops; that, beſides the above, there is alſo an appointment of a *Muſter Maſter General* in North America. This office becoming vacant in 1778, Lord North gave it to one of his friends in the army in *Ireland.* This gentleman has received *five hundred pounds* equipage money, and *two pounds per day,* as we find in the extraordinaries for that year; and yet he never ſtirred out of the kingdom. Lord North explained this to the Houſe of Commons pleaſantly enough, by ſaying that the Commander in Chief in Ireland declared he could not part with ſo excellent an officer.

4th. In 1766 (a time of profound peace) the office of *ſuperintendant* of the *recruiting* ſervice was *created* by Lord Barrington, at *ſeventeen ſhillings per day.* This office is now raiſed to *one pound ten ſhillings per day.* Beſides which, the *contingencies* (which were ſcarce ever juſtifiable) have increaſed

increased from small beginnings to a sum little short of *eight hundred pounds per annum.* The present possessor of this office has also added to the expence by appointing *assistants*, who are paid by the *public*, and has had besides several *thousand* pounds passing through his hands, which have never been accounted for to Parliament.

5th. A foreigner in our service (who certainly had for many years received his full share of appointments as a general officer) was in 1776 appointed *Inspector General* of the forces in the *West-Indies* at *three pounds per day.*——This *new* office was in its nature nearly a *sinecure:* because its various functions were incompatible with each other.——He was never ordered to his post, though he received pay in 1776, and down to September 1777, when he was appointed Governour of Canada.—— He is there in fact confined to the mere defence of the Colony; yet his pay and appointments as Governour have not been deemed sufficient; and he also receives *ten pounds per day* as *Commander in* Chief.

6th.

6th. A *Deputy Commiſſary*, or *Deputy Quarter Maſter General* here in England, at *ten ſhillings per day*, charges *contingencies* very near *double* his pay.

7th. The Hoſpital of the grand army in North *America* was, about two years ago, repreſented to be in ſome confuſion for want of a *Superintendant General*. A gentleman who had the direction of that buſineſs in the laſt war in America, and had acquitted himſelf with great credit and honour, was appointed to this office; and even knighted in order to give him conſideration and reſpect in his new and arduous undertaking.——This gentleman in 1778, received *three pounds per day*, and yet has never been ſent out of the kingdom.

8th. The *Receiver General* of the king's revenue in Canada has not been in that province for many years.——His office it is to be preſumed is a mere *ſinecure*. But the *extraordinaries* of the *army* ſhew—(not what he has *paid* in, as *receiver* of the king's revenue in Canada; but)——that he has

And Contingent Bills.

has *received seven thousand pounds* from the king's Treasury here, to enable him (the *Receiver* of the king's revenue in Canada) to carry on *payments* at Quebec.

This last is too ridiculous! And can only be accounted for by those who know who the gentleman is, who fills this important office, and the nature of his claim to *public* favour.

N. B. The preceding Section V. of this chapter shews, that the *Governours* themselves have not been idle or remiss in making *payments:* and the appointment of such collateral assistants (as this *Receiver* of *Payments!*) carries upon the face of it a very suspicious complexion.

9th. A gentleman is appointed in 1776 *Commissary General* of Stores in England, at *two pounds per day*. The same person is paid as *Engineer*—as *Superintendant* of the batteries on the coasts—and as *Deputy Quarter Master General*.

The

The duties of these different employments seem to be incompatible with each other, but we are taught by the account of the *Extraordinaries*, that they are not intirely so: for he charges *contingencies* as Deputy Quarter Master General, in the years 1776, 1777, and 1778.—One article of payment to this gentleman is of a far more alarming nature than the rest. It stands nakedly thus in the last Account of Extraordinaries:——

—— " *Expence of the Com-*
" *missariat from the opening*
" *of the campaign to De-*
" *cember,* 1778   —— £.1,266."

A Commissariat is a many-headed monster. The establishment of it *at home* is yet in its infancy. The vigour and the vigilance of the Parliament and Public should be called upon at least to check its growth, since they omitted (what would have been much better) to strangle the monster at its birth.

It is a fact, the truth of which cannot be disputed, that the greater the number of of Commissaries, Comptrollers, Intendants, Super-intendants, &c. which are employed, the more money is wasted, the fewer satisfactory accounts are produced, and the more the public interest is neglected.—As one proof of this, let us turn our eyes for a moment to North America. The Commissariat there is said by some to stand at above 30,000*l. per annum*. By others it is said to exceed greatly that sum. The Minister says, that *some* Commissaries, &c. are appointed here by the *Treasury*; others are appointed by the different *Commanders in Chief* abroad; and that the *Commissary General* in North America has himself also a right to appoint as many as he pleases.

What an alarming power is here of creating *new offices* from *five shillings* to *five pounds per day* !

We have been told in Parliament by a gentleman who served lately in that country, that the Commissary General in America declared that near a score of the Commissaries sent to him from England, were then

then totally useless; he had no employment for them, though they were all receiving considerable salaries from Government *(a)*.——For this amazing expence it will naturally be asked, What satisfactory accounts, or what accounts of any sort have been laid before Parliament?—The answer is—*None.*

It is worth stating here that some of the ablest and most intelligent officers in the service, who acted in the last as well as the present war in America, have declared that all this business of the commissariat was managed in the last war by *two* commissaries only, at *one* pound *per day* each: and the Army was far more ably served than it has been lately or now is served, with the enormous charge abovementioned.

If the nation was really in a situation to afford the money thus profusely wasted, yet

---

(a) The Secretary of War, Mr. Jenkinson, has however acquainted the House of Commons in the present session, that there is a saving in the American Estimate of *one pound ten shillings per day* by the death of —— *one* Commissary

And Contingent Bills. 83

yet it ought to be applied to wife and falutary purpofes. A proper diftribution of it would give energy to a fervice in which the inferior officer either fpends his private patrimony or feels the moft poignant diftrefs; the Lieutenant General has appointments inadequate to his high fituation; and the Major General muft either ruin his family or adopt a narrow œconomy very unbecoming his rank.

After the many inftances of marked profufion ftated in the above articles, the reader is defired to turn his attention to the following, out of numberlefs inftances of a different œconomy, in former accounts of extraordinaries of the Army at different periods.

In 1714, (a year of rebellion.)

		l.
For intelligence to the Duke of Athol	—	300
For ditto to others	—	100
For ditto to others	—	20
For ditto to others	—	5
Tranfporting a train of artillery from Edinburgh to Stirling	—	25

To contractors for horses held in readiness — 299 *l.*

In 1740, In an account of transport expences amounting to 105,275*l.* the salary of the Agent and his Clerk is — 328

In 1746, in the extraordinaries, Mr. Reid is paid for his trouble in examining Forage Accounts — 30

In 1756, the expences of two Captains sent as Hostages from Minorca to France — 211

In 1759, General Conway (in a public character) for travelling and incidental expences, to Sluys, to settle a cartel — 200

In 1760, General Watson, Quarter Master General, for settling and visiting the camps in Great Britain — 103

In 1761, General Watson for the same service — 113

We might here, without any trouble, point out a true but moſt invidious contraſt between the above articles in former Extraordinaries, and articles for ſimilar ſervices in the Extraordinaries for the four laſt years. But we have already in this ſection felt great concern in being obliged to allude to many officers, who in other reſpects are men of merit and diſtinction in the ſervice, and though their names appear in the *Extraordinaries,* which are not only printed in the journals of Parliament, but are alſo publiſhed in periodical papers, which circulate throughout the kingdom; yet we forbear to mention their names in this publication, being of opinion that they are not liable to individual or perſonal imputation: For Œconomy in the great line of public expenditure is not ſo much the immediate concern of the private military officer.—When the readineſs to give, becomes known; when a ſyſtem of profuſion is once publickly eſtabliſhed; the blame of all that follows lies principally (if not ſolely) at the door of the *Miniſter.*

N. B. We

N. B. We have taken no notice in this chapter, of an antiquated and repeatedly rejected claim of the Landgrave of Heſſe Caſſel, for Hoſpital Expences in the laſt War, amounting to near 30,000*l.* Parliament, by the advice of the Miniſter, has lately admitted this ſtale claim as a juſt one; but this demand was not ſtated in the Extraordinaries of the Army: it was voted ſeparately.———The Miniſter's love of juſtice however gives all the advantage of a *Nullum Tempus* to every claimant. For we find, in the Extraordinaries of 1774, the diſcharge of debts contracted even in the war before the laſt; viz. 1744, 1745, and 1746.

SECT. VII.

Presents to Indians.

The article of *Presents* to *Indians*, as well on account of the sum, as of its nature and consequences, certainly requires (and will probably one day demand) a more particular account and explanation than can at present be obtained.——It stands briefly thus,

	Through the Under Secretary of State.	By Bills from North America.
In 1775	£. 5,000	
1776	11,000 Guy Johnson,	£. 4,430
1777	12,500 Super Inten-	16,600
1778	25,908 dant *Stuart*	63,306
	————	————
	54,408	84,336
		45,408
Total	————	£. 138,744

In the last war (before the tomahawk and scalping knife were considered as instruments of destruction which God and Nature had put into our hands) these savages

savages were an article of very inconfiderable expence. But now, fince they have had the honour of being our *allies* in the war, they are become far more expenfive to us than any other troops; and have an Agent or Banker appointed for them on each fide of the Atlantic.

The advantages of this *alliance*, the only one which we have cultivated (perhaps becaufe it accorded beft with the principles laid down by our Minifters in the commencement and progrefs of the war) are now thoroughly manifeft——The peaceful inhabitants of the back fettlements, who were all inclined to neutrality, have been forced by the fcalping parties of our Indian allies, to take up the hatchet in their own defence: they have deftroyed the Indian fettlements, and have driven 5000 of them into Niagara, to be fed and fupported by us there till fummer.

The whole *copper race* might eafily have been induced to adopt a neutrality, had not our Minifters prevented it.——God and Nature were faid to juftify our employment of them. But God and Nature now direct them to affist their neighbours againft the more than favage barbarity of their mercilefs invaders.

CHAP. VI.

Ordnance.

THOUGH the account of the ordnance (*i. e.* for artillery, ammunition, &c.) ftands always in a feparate eftimate; yet, being clofely connected with the army, it has been proud of keeping pace with it in the enormity of its expence.

The Ordnance Eftimate voted.

For 1776, is ——	£. 472,827
1777, ——	592,817
1778, ——	683,299
1779, ——	917,373
1780, ——	1,049,602
Total for *five* years —	3,715,918

Compare this with the Ordnance estimates for former wars.

Voted for			
1745	£. 263,435	}	A rebellion in these years.
1746	422,319		
1747	477,213		

Total for 3 years   1,162,967
For 1780   1,049,602

Difference   113,365

Thus it appears that the Ordnance estimates for *three* years (with a rebellion in the country) exceeded the estimate for the single year 1780, only by £. 113,365.

Ordnance estimates of *last* war.

For 1756	——	£. 299,157	}	For the *three* first years £. 1,128,686
1757	——	437,622		
1758	——	391,807		
1759	——	544,277	}	For the *two* next years £. 1,055,137
1760	——	510,860		
1761	——	728,716		
1762	——	642,916		

Total of this war for
seven years — — 3,555,355

By the above account it appears that the expence of the *three* first years of the last war, viz. 1,128,686
exceeded the estimate for the *single* year 1780, which is — 1,049,602

only by the sum of   —   79,084

That

That the *two* next years which were still higher estimated, amounting to — 1,055,137
exceed the estimate of the *single* year 1780, which is — 1,049,602

only by the sum of — 5,535

That the estimate of 1780, which is — — 1,049,602
exceeds the *highest* year of *last* war, viz. — — 728,716

by the sum of — — 320,886

And that the whole expence of Ordnance for *five* years in this war, viz. — — 3,715,918
exceeds the whole expence for *seven* years in the last war, viz. 3,555,355

by the sum of ——— 160,563

This part of the public expenditure is the more worthy of particular examination and controul for the following reasons.

1st. A select Committee of the House of Commons sat in 1763 to examine into the

the conduct of this Board (which it is necessary to observe is merely executive, and bound to obey the higher ministers commands) and reported several very great abuses; especially in the mode of making contracts.

2dly. Above 160 pieces of our cannon were taken in the island of Dominica, where they had not a sufficient guard to take care of them even in a time of profound peace: whilst the valuable island of Jamaica was left totally unprovided with either cannon or ammunition.

3dly. The powder supplied by the Board of Ordnance has been found upon service to be excessively bad.

4thly. A Secretary of State, in a letter to the Commander in Chief in North America, has declared that in the year 1777, this country was left without a single matross for its defence. N. B. A matross is the lowest rank of soldiers in the regiment of artillery.

5thly.

Ordnance. 93

5thly. The arms of several regiments have been reported by the commanding officers of those regiments, to be *unserviceable*.

6thly. It has been stated in Parliament, and has not been denied, that (notwithstanding all these enormous expences) we had not in our great arsenal (the Tower of London) *fifteen thousand* stand of serviceable arms in May 1778; which was two months after the French rescript of war had been presented to our court. This has been attempted to be in some measure accounted for; but in a very aukward manner: for it has been said to arise from the great quantities of arms which have been exported to America: thus proving (besides the improvidence of the measure) that we have been, absurdly as inhumanly, employing our *best* arms against our *friends*, and have now left only the *worst* to cope with our *enemies*.

CHAP.

CHAP. VII.
NAVY DEBT.
(Lord Sandwich's Civil List.)

THE Debt of the Navy arises from money paid by the Admiralty *beyond* the estimates and grants of Parliament. This is not only an intolerable grievance in itself; but has also served as an example which has been latterly but too well copied by the army. And these together are now advancing with such rapid strides, that (unless speedily checked, and that with a very strong hand too, either by Parliament or PEOPLE) they threaten a total subversion of the constitution and an absolute annihilation of the rights of the nation.

The progress of the *Army* extraordinaries has been already exhibited in the Vth Chapter. The progress of the *Navy* Debt (or extraordinaries of the Navy) may be collected from a state of that debt from Christmas 1750 to September 1779; which period including the whole of the last war, will enable the public to compare the commencement of the present war with the commencement of the last.

Navy Debt.

Dec. 31, 1750	-£.	1,716,923
1751	-	1,675,792
1752	-	944,901
1753	-	1,132,106
1754	-	1,296,567
1755	-	1,978,070
1756	-	2,238,009
1757	-	3,462,967
1758	-	4,575,428
1759	-	5,391,830
1760	-	5,228,695
1761	-	5,607,001
1762	-	5,929,124
1763	-	4,046,898
1764	-	3,926,915
1765	-	2,484,595
1766	-	1,456,924
1767	-	1,213,072
1768	-	1,339,158
1769	-	1,082,846
1770	-	1,497,454
1771	-	1,195,409
1772	-	1,535,382
1773	-	1,886,760
1774	-	1,886,100
1775	-	2,698,579
1776	-	3,624,420
1777	-	4,003,573
1778	-	5,179,000
Sep. 30, 1779	-	7,262,415

N.B. In this Account the Debt arising from the Transport Service is included in each year.

Allowing

Allowing 250,000*l. per month* for the three months from September 30 to December 31, 1779. The Navy Debt must now be — — 8,012,415 *l.*

Navy Debt, Dec. 31, 1779   8,012,415 *l.*
The highest year of
last war   5,929,124
Excess at this time 2,083,291

The reader may observe that on the 31st of December 1754, which was the eve of hostilities with France preceding the last war, the Navy debt was - 1,296,567

On the 31st of December 1777, which was the eve of the present hostilities with France, the Navy debt was - - 4,003,573

And that the Navy debt has increased in this last year, i.e. from the 31st of December 1778, to the 31st of December 1779, by the sum of - - 2,833,415

The

The reader will obferve that all this increafe of Navy debt is expended over and above the prodigious eftimates and grants of parliament for the fervice of the navy; and in that very year too, when we have fuffered as a nation difgraces unprecedented in the annals of England. Our coaft has been infulted; the French have been mafters of the Channel: the Mediterranean has been abfolutely deferted: Gibraltar is actually befieged: feveral of our valuable Weft-India iflands have been taken: and the reft either abandoned, or left to a fpecies of defence, which in its confequences muft be almoft as fatal to them as if they had been conquered by France.

From this enormous *civil lift* of the navy, as from a copious fource, flow all thofe abufes which have been fo loudly complained of. Although that complaint has only ferved to drive the firft Lord of the Admiralty for fhelter to a quarter, from whence he has been hitherto enabled to infult the nobleft profeffion in our ifland, and to deride and set at nought all civil and military censure.

To this shelter and to that confidence of security in the first Lord of the Admiralty, which arises from the power and influence in his possession; must we attribute the following notorious abuses:

Ships commissioned for months before they are in readiness; thereby imposing a needless expence both of officers and men upon the nation:

Ships fitted out as fire-ships and new officers appointed to them, although in so deplorable a state that it is impossible for them to venture on the ocean:

Ships purchased of contractors; particularly East-India ships, notoriously unfit for service:

Ships of the line and others kept in pay, although absolutely useless; thereby occasioning both loss and deception to the public:

The practice of purchasing large quantities of foreign timber continued, although the ships which have been repaired with it at an enormous expence could do little or no service afterwards:

The charge of Contractors at the rate of 5 per cent. for fees at the yards and offices:

Partialities shewn by various management to Members of Parliament; and goods over and beyond the contracts, received, although not wanted:

The appointment of new Surveyors of Woods in North America, with a train of attendant expences, under pretence of preserving the timber appropriated to the king's use; though at the same time contracts are making in the very same provinces with private persons:

Parading visitations of the king's yards attended with great immediate expence, loss of time to the workmen, and the delay of important expeditions:

A late lavish and unnecessary grant to the Commissioners of the Navy; who have had an *increase* of salary of *three hundred pounds* a year each; which makes them equal to the Board of Admiralty; and this for conducting the business of the army transports and victuallers, though the trouble bears no proportion to the reward:

Large sums appropriated contrary to the standing orders of the Navy for *Contingencies* of offices:

The scandalous abuse of the Commissioners of the Navy selling their clerkships—a practice big with mischief, and yet so inveterate that a late extraordinary transaction has not been able to produce a remedy:

The practice of Protections which is a great grievance to the mercantile part of the nation; the fees for which, if they must be retained ought at least to be applied to the use of the public:

Large sums of money suffered to remain in the hands of all the accounting officers; such

such as the Treasurer of the Navy, the Paymaster of the Marines, &c. Some of whom have money remaining in their hands even after their accounts are passed, instead of being obliged to make up their ballance at the end of every year, and to pass their accounts at stated periods both at home and abroad; by which means the ballance would come to be expended before more money would be advanced.

N. B. We have here mentioned only some of the notorious abuses in the civil management of the Navy. A very different list would appear upon a thorough investigation made by an honest Committee of Accounts; who would be enabled to unlock the doors of office and penetrate into secrets, the care of concealing which (by their neglect of greater objects) seems to be the chief occupation of those who keep the keys.

CHAP.

CHAP. VIII.

Remarks on Lord North's Method of raising Money by Loans.

AFTER having thus, in the 4th, 5th, 6th, and 7th chapters briefly exhibited the profusion which prevails, under the present Administration, in the *expenditure* of the public money; it will be proper to take a short view of the profuse and ruinous terms on which the *borrowed* money is *raised*.

Scheme of the Loan for 1779.

	l.
Seven millions stock in the 3 per cent. annuities sold at 60 per cent.	4,200,000
Three douceurs, consisting of the profits of a Lottery, a quarter's interest and annuity, and an annuity for 29 years of 3¾ per cent. (i. e. 262,500*l.*) all sold to the Money-lenders for the sum of	2,800,000
Sum advanced	7,000,000

True

of raising Money by Loans. 103

True Value of the Douceurs.

Value of 262,500*l. per ann.*
for 29 years (reckoning interest
at 5 per cent.) is $15\frac{14}{100}$ years
purchase; or   - - 3,974,000

Profits of the Lottery and a
quarter's interest and annuity - 0,260,000
          ——————
          4,234,000

Gained by the Money-lenders, or lost by the Public in this Bargain.

By seven millions stock sold
at 40 per cent. discount *(a)* - 2,800,000

By the Douceurs; being the
difference between 2,800,000*l.*
(the sum paid for them) and
4,234,000*l.* (their true value) 1,432,000
          ——————
    Total loss - 4,232,000
          That

It is necessary to remember here, that when stock is sold, an obligation is incurred to return 100*l.* in money for every 100*l.* stock: and that the public will undoubtedly find itself under a necessity of fulfilling this obligation, should the public debts be ever put into a fixed course of redemption.

104 *Remarks on Lord North's Method*

That the true value of an annuity for 29 years, is $15\frac{14}{100}$ years purchase (when interest is at 5 per cent. or when the 3 per cents. are at 60) may be proved in the following manner.

If any sum is laid out in purchasing such an annuity at this price, *5 per cent. per annum* may be taken as the interest of the principal, and a surplus will be left which in 29 years will accumulate to the principal. For example, with a thousand pounds may be purchased 66*l.* of the annuity, supposing the price $15\frac{14}{100}$ years purchase: 50 pounds *per ann,* may be spent as the interest of the principal at 5 per cent, and the remaining 16*l. per annum* if saved, will in 29 years accumulate to a thousand pounds.

It may seem incredible, but it is true, that though this annuity is thus demonstrably worth $15\frac{14}{100}$ years purchase, when the 3 per cents are at 60: yet Lord North made the public sell it at $9\frac{}{10}$ years purchase; which is the proper price of this annuity when interest is at $9\frac{1}{2}$ per cent, or when the 3 per cents are at 32 —— So that

that the money lender might make $9\frac{1}{2}$ per cent *per annum* interest for the sum he advanced for it, and at the same time secure his purchase money.

The extravagance of the terms of the last loan may therefore be otherwise represented in the following manner.

Procured at 5 per cent, with an obligation to return 100*l*. for every 60*l*. received	4,200,000
Procured at $9\frac{1}{2}$ per cent. (being the purchase money for 262,500 *per annum* for 29 years at $9\frac{7}{10}$ years purchase.	2,540,000
Procured by lottery tickets and a quarter's interest and annuity in advance ———	260,000
	7,000,000

Borrowing 4,200,000*l*. at 5 per cent; and 2,540,000 at $9\frac{1}{2}$ per cent is nearly the same as if the two sums united had been

been borrowed at an interest of 6¼ per cent. This therefore (or 6¼ per cent.) is the interest at which Lord North borrowed money last year: creating at the same time an artificial debt of 2,800,000*l.* which must be paid (if the public debt is ever paid) though *nothing* has been received for it.

Is it possible that a kingdom, already so overloaded, should go on long in borrowing on such terms?

But the terms of the next loan are likely to be still more extravagant: for, it is said, that ten millions in money are to be procured by selling ten millions of 3 per cent. stock at 58 (i. e. for 5,800,000*l.*); an annuity for 28 years of 400,000*l.* for 3,900,000*l.* and the profits of a Lottery and a quarter's advance of the interests and annuity for 300,000*l.*

Should these be the terms, the loss to the public will be;

of raising Money by Loans. 107

By ten millions stock sold at
58 (i. e. 42 per cent. discount). 4,200,000
By the difference between six
millions (the true value *(a)* of
an annuity for 28 years of
400,000*l.*) and 3,900,000*l.* (the
sum paid for it). — 2,100,000

Total loss . 6,300,000

Thus will the Minister, by one bargain, squander away above *six millions*. And this waste is the more to be lamented, because it is unnecessary. For regulations have been proposed *(b)* which would enable Government to borrow always nearly at the rate of interest which money bears in the 3 per cents, *without any douceurs*; and therefore without subjecting the public to the loss it suffers by *douceurs*, and to the necessity of paying at redemption many millions which it never received.

Suppose for instance that in consequence of such regulations, Government (instead

---

(a) This value is very nearly 15 years purchase, reckoning interest at 5 per cent.

(b) See *Supplement* to the *Additional Observations* on *Civil Liberty.*

of borrowing ten millions at $6\frac{1}{4}$ per cent, as it is likely to do) should be able to borrow at $5\frac{1}{4}$; an *annual* charge would in this case be saved of 125,000*l.* besides above *four millions* at redemption.

It will be said indeed that Money-lenders are capricious and greedy, and cannot be induced to lend on cheaper terms.—If this is true, it only proves that the nation is become a prey to rapacious Money-lenders and an extravagant Minister; who between them are wasting its treasure and compleating its ruin: but it will by no means justify the extravagance here represented.

It should not be said that any regulations will not succeed, until some trial has been made of them. And the expences of the nation are now so enormous, that a minister must be inexcusable who does not try every expedient that may produce any saving.

But waving all regard to these regulations, and taking things just as they are, it is easy to show that by only offering the
Long

Long Annuity now at market, as the *douceur*, inftead of the Short Annuity, great favings may be made.—The Long Annuity is now bought and fold at 18 years purchafe; which is the price it ought to bear reckoning intereft at 5¼ per cent.—Let it be fuppofed to be taken as low as 16¼ years purchafe; which is nearly the price it ought to bear reckoning intereft at 6 per Cent.—By felling it at this price Ten Millions might be procured on the following terms,

Ten Millions 3 per cent. Stock fold at 58 ———— 5,800,000

A Long Annuity of 2¼ per cent. or £.237,500 fold at 16¼ ———— ———— 3,900,000

Lottery, and a quarter's intereft and annuity ———— 300,000

£. 10,000,000

By this fcheme Ten Millions would be borrowed at lefs than an Intereft of 5½ per Cent.—The Fund to be provided, would be £.537,500.—And the excefs of the value

value of the Annuity, above the sum paid for it would be nearly £.700,000. Whereas, in consequence of the preference given to a *Short Annuity*, the same sum cannot be borrowed under an interest of 6 ¼ per cent.—A Fund must be provided that will produce £.700,000.— And the excess of the value of the annuity above the sum advanced for it, is no less (as already has been shown) than £.2,100,000.

A minister who either makes contracts or borrows money on higher terms than are necessary is a nuisance to his country.— Some persons think that Lord North does not really know that the *Short Annuity* is so monstrously undervalued as it is; and that this ignorance is the reason of the preference he gives to it.—His *Friends* charitably think that by this preference he means at the end of 28 years to secure a handsome saving for the Sinking Fund, in order to expedite its future operations in discharging our debts.—But his enemies believe that he means by it to provide a saving that shall hereafter strengthen the

Influence

Influence of the Crown and increafe the powers of *Corruption*. Perhaps the founder opinion may be, that both his friends and his enemies are miftaken in their conjectures. Moft probably he does not carry his views fo far forward as to the end of 28 years *(a)* a period which (if our affairs continue but a little longer under his management) is likely to exceed confiderably the duration of the Funds.

(a) Lord Hillfborough (if we may judge from his declaration in the Houfe of Lords on the 15th of laft December) feems to entertain the *founder opinion*; and to be one of thofe who have not the ftrongeft perfuafion in the world of Lord North's *providence:* for Lord Hillfborough did then folemnly affert it to be his firm belief, that if Lord North fhould quit his poft as minifter to-morrow, he would not be able to maintain his family.—How well this modeft affertion of Lord Hillfborough accords with Lord North's repeated declaration of a willingnefs and defire to refign his office; and how it can be reconciled with the other lucrative appointments of himfelf and his family, the reader is left to determine. However at the worft, with the affiftance of Mr. Atkinfon and the other contractors, his Secretary Mr. Robinfon will have wherewithal to maintain both his own family and his Lordfhip's.

CON-

CONCLUSION.

To the Landholders, &c.

Fellow Countrymen,

IN the preceding Pages we have laid before you some few notorious and incontestable Facts (which lie merely on the threshold of inquiry) selected from a numerous Host of others of the same nature.

It may perhaps be unnecessary here to suggest two important reflections to the attentive reader;

1st. That we have in this publication confined ourselves merely to the *Expenditure* of the public money; and have avoided to take notice of the shameful abuses which prevail in the *Receipt* of the revenue and in the *manner of accounting* for it. The waste and plunder of the public money under these heads are not of a less magnitude or of smaller importance than the abuses in the Expenditure. But they deserve a separate discussion, and shall have it; if it shall appear that the intelligence here communicated is welcome to the public, and serves at all to rouse them

to

to a sense of their wrongs, and to resolutions of obtaining justice.

2dly. That, in this publication, the profusion, mismanagement, and corrupt influence and practices of the present ministers are exhibited only by way of *comparison* with the conduct and practices of all former ministers in this country, even the most wasteful, incapable, corrupt, and inattentive. We have here given to you only a *comparative* view of present with former abuses: thus allowing to our present government the *vantage* ground of all the improper practices and impositions, which have been gradually (though not insensibly) stealing upon the kingdom in the administration of the executive branch of the legislature, from the time of the revolution down to his present Majesty's accession to the throne of the discarded Stuarts.——What these progressive abuses must necessarily be in the course of near a century, the most uninformed politician may easily conjecture. They who are better informed in these matters, see with an indignation which forbids all moderate expreſſions, that that influence of the crown and power of corruption (ſo progreſſively augmented) which have been thought more than ſufficient for all the purpoſes (whether proper or improper) of all former adminiſtrations; inſtead of ſatisfying the inordinate appetite of theſe miniſters of deſpotiſm, have only imparted to them the daring confidence of ſtill farther augmenting that corruption to ſo ſcandalous a degree, that if his Majeſty ſhould now chuſe to promote his poſtilion, or (with the Roman Emperor) his *Horſe* to the office of Firſt Lord of the Treaſury, his neigh would be attended by as great a *majority* as that which now follows the heels of the preſent noble Lord in poſſeſſion *(a)*.

(a) Mr. SMELT, in his known ſituation, has been ſo impolitic as to avow an opinion that the king has not power enough, and that the influence of the crown ought to be ſtill farther augmented. To thoſe who know the man and his communication, this is an awful warning indeed!

God forbid that his Majeſty (of whoſe royal favour and confidence Mr. Smelt poſſeſſes ſo diſtinguiſhed and conſiderable a ſhare) ſhould himſelf entertain any opinion of the ſame nature. Moſt miſerable indeed would
then

If, in this your alarming situation, many words are necessary to excite you to vigorous and decisive exertions, we have already survived the liberties of our country. The corrupt *influence of the Crown* is risen to such a height, that it will not be sufficient merely to *clip* the wings with which it mounted; they must be *seared* to prevent their putting forth again. We are now arrived at a period when either corruption must be thoroughly purged from the Senate, or the nation is finally and irrecoverably undone. If no remaining remedy can be found, by which this pestilence may be quietly removed—*Actum est de Republica*. Let us fix the mark of the plague upon the doors of the house, and then——Let him that will die of the infection, enter.

---

then be the condition of his subjects, and still more miserable that of his Majesty: for *they* might still have hope; but *he* would be compelled (having all) to sit down with Alexander and weep for other worlds to conquer.

[116]

The following is a lift of the noble lords who (by their votes on the two firſt motions recited in the beginning of this publication) are confidered with the utmoſt gratitude by the public as irrevocably pledged to their country for the effectual profecution of a thorough and fpeedy reformation.

Dukes of	Cumberland	*Earls of*	Jerſey
	Bolton		Radnor
	Devonſhire		Shelburne
	Grafton		Spencer
	Mancheſter		Suffolk
	Portland		Tankerville
	Richmond		Courtney
	Rutland	*Viſcounts*	Hereford
Marquis of	Rockingham		Say and Seal
Earls of	Abingdon		Townſhend
	Beſsborough		Abergavenny
	Chatham	*Lords*	Beaulieu
	Cholmondely		Craven
	Coventry		Forteſcue
	Derby		King
	Effingham		Pagett
	Egremont		Ravenſworth
	Ferrers		St. John
	Fitzwilliam		St. Aſaph
	Gainſborough	*Biſhops of*	Peterborough
	Harcourt		

The following is a list of the noble lords who voted for the THIRD motion, made by Lord Shelburne Feb. 8, 1780.

Dukes of	Cumberland	*Earls of*	Tankerville
	Bolton		Temple
	Devonshire	*Viscount*	Courtney
	Grafton		Hereford
	Manchester	*Lords*	Abergavenny
	Portland		Beaulieu
	Richmond		Camden
	Rutland		Craven
Marquis of	Carmarthen		De Ferrars
	Rockingham		Fortescue
Earls of	Abingdon		King
	Berkley		Monson
	Besborough		Pagett
	Cholmondely		Ravensworth
	Coventry		Romney
	Derby		St. John
	Effingham		Walpole
	Egremont	*Bishops of*	St. Asaph
	Ferrers		Peterborough
	Fitzwilliam		
	Harborough	*Unable, through infirmity, to stay for the division*	
	Harcourt		
	Jersey	*Earl of* Strafford	
	Northington	*Bishop of* Carlisle	
	Pembroke		
	Radnor	*Voted by Proxy*	
	Scarborough	*Earl*	Chatham
	Shelburne		Spencer
	Stamford	*Viscount*	Torrington
	Stanhope	*Lords*	Chedworth
	Suffolk		Foley

FINIS.

www.ingramcontent.com/pod-product-compliance
Lightning Source LLC
Chambersburg PA
CBHW020131170426
43199CB00010B/723